A

MOTHER'S

JOURNAL

# A MOTHER'S JOURNAL

*A Book of Days*

Museum of Fine Arts, Boston

© 1991 Museum of Fine Arts, Boston
All rights reserved.

ISBN 0-87846-338 (MFA)
ISBN 0-8212-1886-7 (Bulfinch Press)

First published in 1991 by
The Museum of Fine Arts, Boston
and Bulfinch Press
Bulfinch Press is an imprint and trademark
of Little, Brown and Company (Inc.)

Published simultaneously in Canada by
Little, Brown and Company (Canada) Limited

Produced by the Department of Retail Publications
Museum of Fine Arts, Boston
Project coordinator: Kathryn Sky-Peck
Production coordinator: Lori Stein, Layla Productions

PRINTED AND BOUND IN HONG KONG

THIS BOOK
BELONGS TO:

.......................................

*1*

*2*

anuary

*3*

*Children are the anchors
that hold a mother to life.*
SOPHOCLES, *PHAEDRA*

4

5

6

7

*Caritas*, 1894–1895
Abbott Handerson Thayer (American 1849–1921)
Oil on canvas, 84 ½ x 54 ⅝ inches
Warren Collection & contributions through
Paint & Clay Club.
97.199

8

*Ellen Mary in a White Coat,* about 1896
Mary Stevenson Cassatt (American 1844–1926)
Oil on canvas, 34 ¼ x 24 inches
Anonymous Fractional Gift in Honor
of Ellen Mary Cassatt.
1982.630

9

11

10

12

*A prudent mother will not
clothe her little Childe
with a long and cumbersome
garment.*

ANNE BRADSTREET

13

14

15

16

17

18

19

*Happy he
With such a mother! faith in woman
Beats with his blood, and
trust in all things high
Comes easy to him.*

ALFRED, LORD TENNYSON, "THE PRINCESS"

*The Little Convalescent*, about 1873–1879
Jonathan Eastman Johnson (American 1824–1906)
Oil on academy board, 12 ½ x 11 inches
Frederick Brown Fund.
40.90

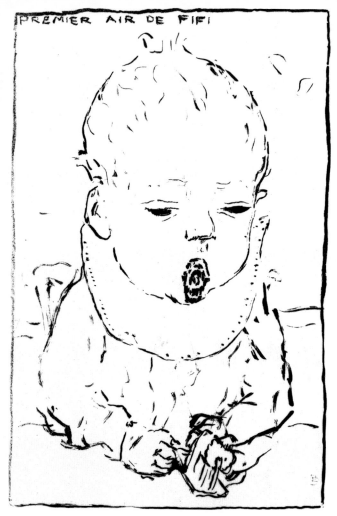

"Premier air de Fifi," from *Petites Scènes Familiares*, 1893
Pierre Bonnard (French 1867–1947)
Lithograph, 6¾ x 4⅜ inches (image)
Lee M. Friedman Fund.
66.365

20

21

22

23

24

25

26

*A baby is a misshapen creature
of no particular age, sex,
or condition, chiefly remarkable
for the violence of the sympathies
and antipathies it excites in others,
itself without sentiment or emotion.*

AMBROSE BIERCE, *THE DEVIL'S DICTIONARY*

January

27

28

29

30

31

> *The very highest function of woman is to raise and train the family. It is the very highest function of man also.*
>
> MARY ASHTON RICE LIVERMORE, *WHAT SHALL WE DO WITH OUR DAUGHTERS*

*The Daughters of Edward D. Boit*, 1882
John Singer Sargent (American  1856–1925)
Oil on canvas, 87⅝ x 87⅝ inches
Gift of Mary Louisa Boit, Julia Overing Boit, Jane Hubbard Boit, and Florence D. Boit in memory of their father, Edward Darley Boit.
19.124

**1**

**2**

**4**

*ebruary*

**3**

**5**

*A man who has been the indisputable favorite of his mother keeps for life the feeling of a conqueror, that confidence of success that often inspires real success.*

SIGMUND FREUD, *LETTERS*

*6*

*Mother and Son*, 1915
Egon Schiele (Austrian 1890–1918)
Black crayon, watercolor, gouache, pencil
19 x 12 ½ inches
Edwin E. Jack Fund.
65.1322

# February

## 7

## 8

## 9

## 10

## 11

## 12

*You may have tangible wealth untold*
*Caskets of jewels and coffers of gold*
*Richer than I you can never be—*
*I had a mother who read to me.*
STRICKLAND GILLILAN, "THE READING MOTHER"

*Reading Lesson*, 1865
Auguste Toulmouche (French 1829–1890)
Oil on canvas, 14 3/8 x 10 7/8 inches
Gift of Francis A. Foster.
24.1

*Annie Seated*, about 1858
James A. McNeill Whistler (American 1834–1903)
Etching and drypoint on pale green
paper, 5⅛ x 3¾ inches
Gift of Weston P. and Rebecca P. Figgins.
1984.880

**13**

**14**

**15**

*Sometimes she still swims
at my center;
sometimes she is a four-year-old
an ocean away
and I am on vertiginous terrain
where I am nobody's mother
and nobody's daughter.*

Marilyn Hacker, "La Fontaine De Valcluse"

16

18

17

19

*Kneeling in an Armchair,* 1904
Mary Stevenson Cassatt (American 1844–1926)
Drypoint, 11 7/8 x 9 1/2 inches
Gift of Perry T. Rathbone.
55.900

# February

## 20

## 21

*Nobody can have the soul of me.*
*My mother has had it, and nobody*
*can have it again. Nobody can come*
*into my very self again, and breathe*
*me in like an atmosphere.*

D.H. Lawrence, *Selected Letters*

## 22

## 23

## 24

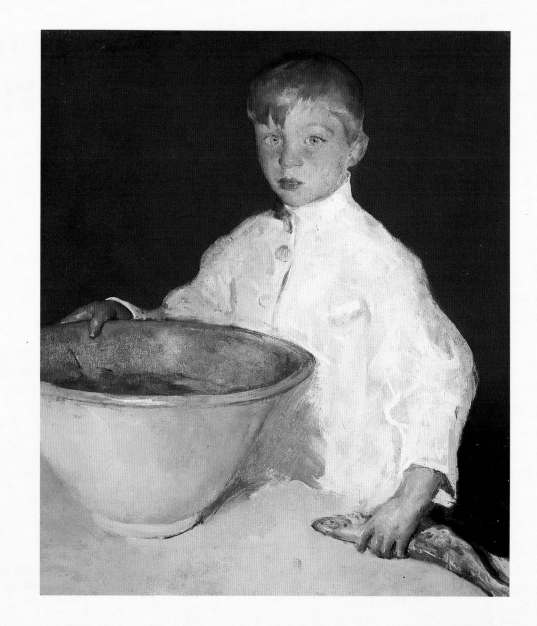

*The Bowl*, 1898
Charles W. Hawthorne (American 1872–1930)
Oil on canvas, 30 x 25 inches
Gift of Frederick L. Jack.
35.1222

# February

## 26

## 27

## 28

## 29

> *Every time we teach a child something, we keep him from inventing it by himself.*
>
> JEAN PIAGET

*Child in Lamplight,* 1897
Pierre Bonnard (French 1867–1947)
Color lithograph, 13 x 18 inches (image)
Bequest of W.G. Russell Allen.
60.67

# 1

# 2

# 4

# *March*

*A baby is God's opinion
that the world should go on.*

CARL SANDBURG

# 3

# 5

**6**

**7**

*Baby Reaching* (Study for *Offering Baby a Top)*
James Goodwyn Clonney (American  1812–1867)
Brush and brown wash,  5 ½ x 7 ⁵⁄₁₆ inches
The M. and M. Karolik Collection.
62.219

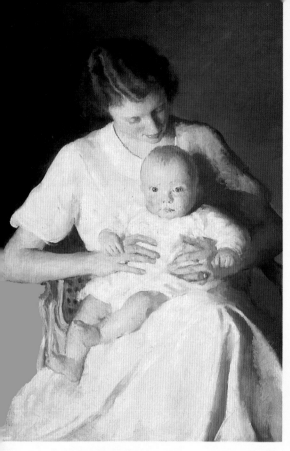

*Mother and Child*
Marie Danforth Page (American 1869–1940)
Oil on canvas, 45 1/4 x 34 1/4 inches
Gift of Erville Maynard.
1980.262

8

9

10

11

*Love me—I love you*
*Love me, my baby.*
*Sing it high, sing it low.*
*Sing it as it may be.*

*Mother's arms under you.*
*Her eyes above you.*
*Sing it high, sing it low.*
*Love me—I love you.*
CHRISTINA ROSSETTI

12

13

14

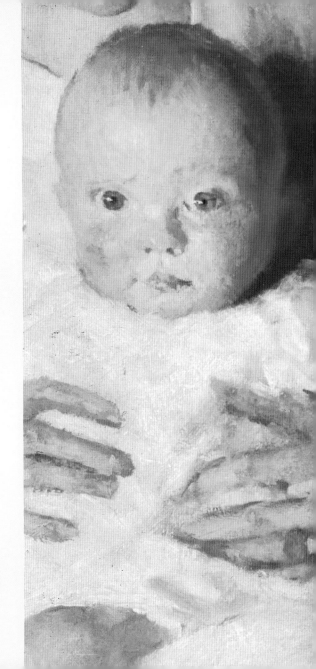

March

15

16

17

18

19

20

*Your clear eye is the one
absolutely beautiful thing
I want to fill it with
colors and ducks
The zoo of the new*
SYLVIA PLATH, "CHILD"

*Jacques Bergeret as a Child*
Pierre Auguste Renoir (French 1841–1919)
Oil on canvas, 16 ⅛ x 12 ⅝ inches
Bequest of John T. Spaulding.
48.595

*Head of a Baby,* **before 1891**
Mary Stevenson Cassatt (American 1844–1926)
Pastel on paper, 14 x 12 inches
Gift of Mrs. Richard Storey in memory of her
mother, Mrs. Bayard Thayer.
62.340

22

23

24

26

*Every beetle is a gazelle
in the eyes of its mother.*
MOORISH PROVERB

25

27

28

# March

**30**

**29**

**31**

*Ah, lucky girls who grow up
in the shelter of a mother's love.*

Edith Wharton

*Emma and Her Children*, 1923
George Wesley Bellows (American 1882–1925)
Oil on canvas, 59 x 65 inches
Gift of Subscribers and
John Lowell Gardner Fund.
25.105

*1*

*2*

*4*

April

*3*

*5*

I, who was never quite sure
About being a girl, needed another
life and another image to
remind me . . .
I made you to find me.

ANNE SEXTON, "THE DOUBLE IMAGE"

*6*

*Gertrude,* 1899
Frank Weston Benson (American 1862–1951)
Oil on canvas, 50 x 40 inches
Gift of Mrs. William Rodman Fay.
54.596

7

*Mrs. Fiske Warren (Gretchen Osgood) and Her Daughter, Rachel*, 1903
John Singer Sargent (American 1856–1925)
Oil on canvas, 59 x 39 3/8 inches
Gift of Mrs. Rachel Warren Barton &
Emily L. Ainsley Fund.
64.693

8

10

9

11

12

*Thou art thy mother's glass,*
*and she in thee*
*Calls back the lovely April*
*of her prime*

WILLIAM SHAKESPEARE, "SONNET 3"

April

13

"Natural History," from *Rhymes of Real Children* (New York, 1913)
Jessie Wilcox Smith (American 1863–1935)
Color relief, 8½ x 7¾ inches
Anonymous Gift.

14

15

16

17

18

19

20

The greatest poem ever known
Is one all poets have outgrown:
The poetry, innate, untold,
Of being only four years old.

CHRISTOPHER MORLEY, "TO A CHILD"

"Kittens," from *Rhymes of Real Children*
(New York, 1913)
Jessie Wilcox Smith (American 1863–1935)
Color relief, 8½ x 7¾ inches
Anonymous Gift.

*Mother and Child,* about 1904
(Julius) Gari Melchers (American 1860–1932)
Pastel on paper, 21 ¼ x 15 ¾ inches
The Hayden Collection 1933.
33.10

## 22

## 24

*Helmer: Before all else you are
a wife and a mother.
Nora: I don't believe that any longer.
I believe that before all else I am a
reasonable human being just
as you are—or, at all events,
I must try and become one.*

HENRIK IBSEN, *A DOLL'S HOUSE*

## 23

## 25

## 26

# April 🙟

## 27

## 28

## 29

## 30

1

2

4

*M*ay

3

5

*Oh, what a power is motherhood,*
*possessing a potent spell*
*All women alike*
*Fight fiercely for a child.*

EURIPIDES, *IPHIGENIA IN AULIS*

6

*Mother and Child*
Mary Stevenson Cassatt (American  1844–1926)
Oil on canvas, 36 ½ x 29 inches
Gift of Miss Aime Lamb in memory of Mr and
Mrs. Horatio A. Lamb.
1970.252

May

7

8

9

10

11

*12*

*A mother who boasts two boys
was ever accounted rich.*

ROBERT BROWNING, "IVAN IVANOVITCH"

*Fraternal Love,* 1851
William Adolphe Bouguereau (French  1825–1905)
Oil on canvas, 57⅞ x 44¾ inches
Gift of the Estate of Thomas Wigglesworth.
08.186

## 17

## 18

## 19

> *There was never a child so lovely*
> *but his mother was glad*
> *to get him to sleep.*
>
> RALPH WALDO EMERSON, *JOURNALS*

*The Artist's Daughter Asleep (facing right)*

*The Artist's Daughter Asleep (facing left)*
Jean Michel Moreau (French 1741–1814)
Pen, black ink, and wash, 4 x 5 5/16 inches
Bequest of Forsyth Wickes,
Forsyth Wickes Collection
65.2592, 65.2593

*Charlotte Nichols Greene and her Son Stephen*, 1924
John Singer Sargent (American 1856–1925)
Charcoal on cream laid paper, 17 ½ x 23 ¾ inches
Gift of Mrs. Stephen Greene.
1986.970

**20**

**21**

## 22

## 24

*All women become like their mothers.*
*That is their tragedy.*
*No man does. That's his.*

OSCAR WILDE, *THE IMPORTANCE OF BEING EARNEST*

## 23

## 25

## 26

# May

## 27

## 28

## 29

## 30

## 31

*A mother is not a person
to lean on but a person
to make leaning unnecessary.*

DOROTHY CANFIELD FISHER

*Woman with a Parasol and a Small Child on
a Sunlit Hillside*, about 1874–1876
Pierre Auguste Renoir (French  1841–1919)
Oil on canvas, 18 ½ x 22 ⅛ inches
Bequest of John T. Spaulding.
48.593

## 1

## 2

## 4

# June

## 3

## 5

*. . . blest the Babe,*
*Nursed in His Mother's arms,*
*who sinks to sleep*
*Rocked on his Mother's breast;*
*who with his soul drinks in*
*the feelings of his Mother's eye!*

WILLIAM WORDSWORTH, *THE PRELUDE*

6

*Venus and Cupid*, about 1800
John Singleton Copley (American 1738–1815)
Oil on panel, 24 ¾ x 20 inches
Bequest of Susan Greene Dexter, in memory of
Charles and Martha Babcock Amory.
25.94

*Maternal Caress*, 1890–1891
Mary Stevenson Cassatt (American 1844–1926)
Drypoint, aquatint, and softground etching
in color, 14 ½ x 10 ⁹⁄₁₆
Gift of William Emerson and Charles Henry
Hayden Fund.
41.808

8

10

*So to be loved, so to be wooed*
*Oh more than mortal*
*woman should!*
*What if she fail*
*or fall behind?*
*Lord, make me worthy,*
*keep them blind.*

KATHERINE TYNAN

9

11

12

13

14

15

16

17

18

*19*

*During the first weeks, I used to lie
long hours with the baby in my arms,
watching her asleep; sometimes
catching a gaze from her eyes:
feeling very near the edge, the mystery,
perhaps the knowledge of life.*

ISADORA DUNCAN, *MY LIFE*

*Flower: Nancy Hale, aged six weeks* (detail)
Lilian Westcott Hale (American 1881–1963)
Charcoal on white board, 23 1/16 x 14 5/16 inches
Gift of Nancy Hale Bowers.
1986.534

20

21

22

23

24

Oh, sacrament of summer days,
Oh, last communion in the haze,
Permit a child to join
EMILY DICKINSON

*Calm Morning*, 1904
Frank Weston Benson (American 1862–1951)
Oil on canvas, 44 x 36 inches
Gift of the Charles A. Coolidge Family.
1985.925

## June

### 26

### 27

### 28

### 29

### 30

*Mankind owes to children
the best it has to give.*

UNITED NATIONS DECLARATION

*Camille Monet and a Child in the Artist's
Garden in Argenteuil*, 1875
Oscar Claude Monet (French 1840–1926)
Oil on canvas, 21 ¾ x 25 ½ inches
Anonymous Gift in Memory of
Mr. and Mrs. Edwin S. Webster.
1976.833

**1**

**2**

**4**

# July

The mother-child relationship is
paradoxical . . . It requires the most
intense love on the mother's side,
yet this very love must help the child
grow away from the mother, and
become fully independent.

ERICH FROMM, *THE SANE SOCIETY*

**3**

**5**

6

*The Drummer Boy,* 1861
William Morris Hunt (American 1824–1879)
Oil on canvas, 36 x 26 inches
Gift of Mrs. Samuel H. Wolcott.
66.1055

*Give a little love to a
child, and you get
a great deal back.*

JOHN RUSKIN, "THE CROWN
OF WILD OLIVE"

*Gathering Fruit,* about 1893
Mary Stevenson Cassatt (American 1844–1926)
Drypoint, softground etching, and aquatint in
color (9th state),  16⅝ x 11¾ inches
Gift of William Emerson and Charles Henry
Hayden Fund.
41.813

8

9

10

11

12

13

# July

## 14

## 15

Cover, from *Rhymes of Real Children*
(New York, 1913)
Jessie Wilcox Smith (American 1863–1935)
Color relief, 11 ½ x 10 ½ inches
Anonymous Gift.

## 16

## 17

*Youth fades, love droops,*
*the leaves of friendship fall;*
*A mother's secret hope*
*outlives them all.*
OLIVER WENDELL HOLMES, "MOTHER'S SECRET"

18

19

20

21

22

*Woman and Child (Au Square)*, 1897
from *L'estampe Moderne*
Henri Jacques Evenepoel (Belgian 1872–1899)
Color lithograph, 13 x 9 inches
Anonymous Gift.

**23**

**25**

*Come along in then, little girl!*
*Or else stay out!*
*But in the open door she stands,*
*And bites her lip and*
*twists her hands,*
*And stares upon me, trouble-eyed:*
*"Mother," she says, "I can't decide!*
*I can't decide!"*

EDNA ST. VINCENT MILLAY,
"FROM A VERY LITTLE SPHINX"

**24**

**26**

**27**

# July

**28**

**29**

**30**

**31**

*The world has no such*
*flowers in any land*
*And no such pearl in any gulf the sea*
*As any babe on any mother's knee.*
ALGERNON CHARLES SWINBURNE, "PELAGIUS"

*Mother and Child in a Boat,* 1892
Edmund C. Tarbell (American 1862–1938)
Oil on canvas, 30⅜ x 35 inches
Bequest of David P. Kimball in Memory of his wife,
Clara Bertram Kimball.
23.532

*1*

*2*

*4*

ugust

*3*

*You who are so beautiful*
*Your deep and childish faces,*
*Your tall bodies—*

*Shall I warn you?*

DENISE LEVERTOV, "THE SUN GOING DOWN UPON
OUR WRATH"

*Three Boys on a Beached Dory,* 1873
Winslow Homer (American 1836–1910)
Black chalk and white watercolor on buff paper
7 x 15 ½ inches
Bequest of the estate of
Katharine Dexter McCormick.
68.575

5

6

7

*Under the Horse Chestnut Tree*, 1896–1897
Mary Stevenson Cassatt (American 1844-1926)
Drypoint and aquatint in color, 15⅞ x 11¼ inches
Bequest of W.G. Russell Allen.
63.313

9

10

11

12

13

*Lord who ordainst for mankind*
*Benignant toils and tender cares*
*We thank thee for the ties that bind*
*The mother to the child she bears.*
WILLIAM CULLEN BRYANT

August

14

15

16

17

18

19

## 20

*You can do anything with children*
*if you only play with them.*
OTTO VON BISMARCK

*Gabrielle and Coco Playing Dominoes*
Pierre Auguste Renoir (French 1841–1919)
Oil on canvas, 20 ½ x 18 ⅛ inches
Given in Memory of Governor Alvan T. Fuller by
the Fuller Foundation.
61.960

## 21

You wish, O woman! to be ardently
loved and forever, even till death.
Be then, the mothers of your children.

JEAN PAUL F. RICHTER, *LEVANA*

*The Bath*, 1890–1891
Mary Stevenson Cassatt (American 1844–1926)
Drypoint, softground etching, and aquatint in color
12 5/8 x 9 3/4 inches
Gift of William Emerson and
Charles Henry Hayden Fund.
41.806

22

23

24

25

26

27

## August

### 28

### 29

### 30

### 31

*Your children are not your children.*
*They are the sons and daughters*
*of Life's longing for itself.*

KAHLIL GIBRAN, "ON CHILDREN"
FROM THE PROPHET

*Boys in a Pasture*, 1874
Winslow Homer (American 1836–1910)
Oil on canvas, 15 ¼ x 22 ½ inches
The Hayden Collection.
53.2552

**1**

**2**

**4**

**S**eptember

**3**

**5**

*Judicious mothers will always keep in mind that they are the first book read, and the last put aside, in every child's library.*

C. Lenox Redmond

*Two Girls Looking at a Book,* about 1880
Winslow Homer (American 1836–1910)
Wash drawing, 5 3/8 x 8 5/8 inches
Bequest of the estate of Katharine Dexter McCormick.
68.572

*September*

6

7

8

9

10

11

Children know the grace of God
Better than most of us.
They see the world
The way the morning brings it
back to them.

ARCHIBALD MACLEISH, *JB*

*Open Air Concert*
Lilla Cabot Perry (American  1848-1933)
Oil on canvas, 40 x 30 inches
Gift of Miss Margaret Perry
64.2055

13

*Ah! happy years! once more
who would not be a boy?*

LORD BYRON, "CHILDE HAROLD'S PILGRIMAGE"

*The Torn Hat*, 1820
Thomas Sully (American 1783–1872)
Oil on panel, 19 x 14 inches
Gift of Belle Greene and Henry Copley Greene, in
memory of their mother, Mary Abby Greene.
16.104

14

16

18

15

17

19

September

20

21

22

23

24

25

## 26

*The best academy, a mother's knee.*

JAMES RUSSELL LOWELL, "THE CATHEDRAL"

*In the Omnibus*, 1890–1891
Mary Stevenson Cassatt (American 1844–1926)
Drypoint and aquatint in color, 14 ⅜ x 10 ½ inches
Gift of William Emerson and
Charles Henry Hayden Fund.
41.805

## September

### 27

### 28

### 29

### 30

*Is not a young mother
one of the sweetest sights
which life shows us?*

WILLIAM MAKEPEACE THACKERAY, *THE NEWCOMES*

*Mother and Child*, 1895
George de Forest Brush (American  1855–1941)
Oil on panel, 40 ⅜ x 39 ½ inches
Warren Collection.
95.1375

*1* _____

*2* _____

*4* _____

# October

*The future destiny of
the child is always
the work of the mother.*

NAPOLEON BONAPARTE

*3* _____

*5* _____

*6*

*The Dandelion Girl (Lydia Bigelow)*, 1877
George Fuller (American 1822–1884)
Oil on canvas, 50 x 40½ inches
Dr. & Mrs. George Faulkner, through the
Trustees of the Faulkner Hospital.
11.2808

7

*Little Rose of Lyme Regis,* 1895
James A. McNeill Whistler (American 1834–1903)
Oil on canvas, 20 ¼ x 12 ⅜ inches
Warren Collection.
96.950

8

9

10

11

12

*If we could start again,*
*You, newbegotten, I*
*A clean stick peeled*
*Of twenty paper layers of years*
*I'd tell you only what you know*
*But barely know you know.*
*Teach one commandment,*
*"Mind the senses and the soul*
*Will take care of itself*
*Being five times blessed."*

ANNE WILKINSON, "LETTER TO MY CHILDREN"

October

13

14

15

16

17

18

*Some are kissing mothers
and some are scolding mothers,
but it is love just the same, and
most mothers kiss and scold together.*

PEARL S. BUCK

"Miss Mariar," from *Rhymes of Real
Children* (New York, 1913)
Jessie Wilcox Smith (American 1863–1935)
Color relief, 8 ½ x 7 ¾ inches
Anonymous Gift.

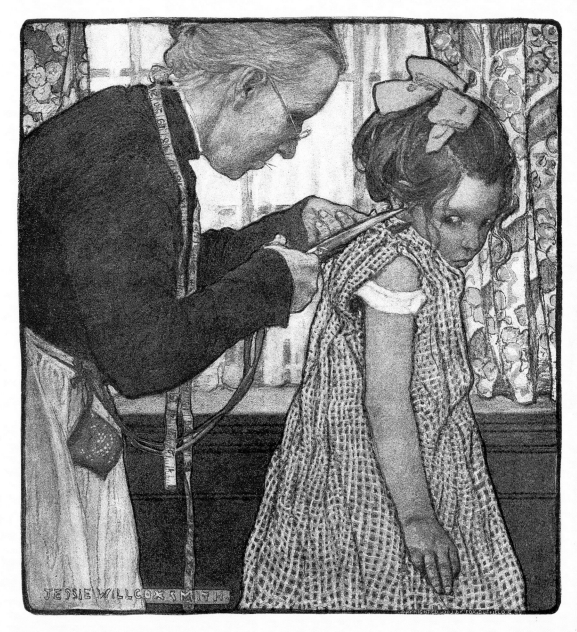

'Tis education
forms the common mind
Just as the twig is bent,
the tree's inclined.

ALEXANDER POPE

*Writing to Father,* 1863
Jonathan Eastman Johnson (American 1824–1906)
Oil on artist's board, 12 x 9¼ inches
Bequest of Maxim Karolik.
64.435

21

22

23

24

25

26

# October

*People murder a child when they tell*
*it to keep out of the dirt.*
*In dirt is life.*

28

30

27

29

31

*Children Playing under a Gloucester Wharf,* 1880
Winslow Homer (American 1836-1910)
Watercolor on paper 8 x 13¼ inches
Hayden Collection, Charles Henry Hayden Fund.
21.2554

1

ovember

2

3

4

5

*Begin, little boy,*
*to recognize your mother*
*by a smile.*
VIRGIL, *ECLOGUES.*

6

*Boy with a Cat*
Anonymous (American 19th century)
Oil on canvas, 34 x 27 inches
Gift of Edgar Williams and
Bernice Chrysler Garbisch.
1981.106

# November

## 7

## 8

## 9

## 10

## 11

## 12

*13*

O' blessed vision! happy child
Thou art so exquisitely wild
I think of thee with many fears
For what may be thy lot
in future years.

WILLIAM WORDSWORTH, "TO HARTLEY COLERIDGE"

*Girl with Cat*, 1856
William Morris Hunt (American  1824-1879)
Oil on canvas, 42 x 33½ inches
Bequest of Edmund Dwight
00.504

14

"When Daddy was a Little Boy."
from *Rhymes of Real
Children* (New York, 1913)
Jessie Wilcox Smith (American  1863–1935)
Color relief, 8½ x 7¾ inches
Anonymous Gift.

**15**

**16**

**17**

**18**

*When Mother smiled her face, beautiful though it was, became infinitely more so, and things seemed to brighten up all around. If I could have caught but a passing glimpse of that smile in the trying moments of my life, I wouldn't have known what sorrow is.*

Leo Tolstoy, Childhood, Boyhood, Youth

**19**

November

20

21

22

23

24

25

*I have a small
daughter called
Cleis, who is
like a golden
flower
I wouldn't
take all Croesus'
kingdom with love
thrown in, for her.*
SAPPHO

*Miss Helen Sears*, 1895
John Singer Sargent (American 1856–1925)
Oil on canvas, 65¾ x 35¾ inches
Gift of Mrs. J.D. Cameron Bradley.
55.1116

# November

**26**

**27**

**28**

**29**

**30**

*Our aim is discipline for
activity, for work, for goals,
not for immobility,
not for passivity,
not for obedience.*

MARIA MONTESSORI

*Three Little Girls in Red*, 1897
Maurice Brazil Prendergast (American 1858–1924)
Monotype, 5 5/8 x 6 inches
George P. Gardner Fund.
55.228

**1**

**2**

**4**

**D**ecember

**3**

**5**

*They all were looking for a king*
*To slay their foes, and lift them high;*
*Thou cam'st, a little baby thing*
*That made a woman cry.*

GEORGE MACDONALD, "THAT HOLY THING"

6

*Virgin and Child*
Domenico Corvi (Italian 1721–1803)
Oil on canvas, 23 5/8 x 19 1/8 inches
Bequest of Mrs. Henry Edwards.
90.76

December *

7

8

9

*Robert de Cèvrieux* , 1879
John Singer Sargent (American  1856–1925)
Oil on canvas, 33 5/8 x 19 inches
The Hayden Collection.
22.372

## 10

## 12

*The God to whom little boys say*
*their prayers has a face*
*very like their mother's.*

Sir James M. Barrie

## 11

## 13

## 14

## December

### 15

### 16

*As is the mother,*
*so is her daughter*

EZEKIAL, XVI, 44

### 17

### 18

### 19

*20*

*Portrait of Georgianna Buckham
and her mother,* 1839
Henry Inman (American  1801–1846)
Oil on canvas, 34 ¼ x 27 ¼ inches
Bequest of Georgianna Buckham Wright.
19.1370

# December

## 21

## 22

## 23

## 24

## 25

*The beautiful mother is bending*
*Low where her baby lies*
*Helpless and frail, for her tending;*
*But she knows the glorious eyes.*

*The mother smiles, rejoices*
*While the baby laughs in the hay;*
*She listens to heavenly voices:*
*"The child shall be king one day."*

SOPHIE JEWETT (FROM THE LATIN OF
JACOPONE DA TODI), "NATIVITY SONG"

## 26

*Virgin and Child*
Luis de Morales (Spanish about 1509–1586)
Oil on panel, 18 ⅛ x 13 ⅝ inches
Gift of Misses Aime and Rosamond Lamb.
1978.680

# December

## 27

## 28

## 29

## 30

## 31

*In every child who is born, under no matter what circumstances, and of no matter what parents, the potentiality of the human race is born again.*

JAMES AGEE

*Boston Common at Twilight,* 1885–1886
Childe Hassam (American 1859–1935)
Oil on canvas, 42 x 60 inches
Gift of Miss Maud E. Appleton.
31.952